D1413624

Voices from the American Revolution

LEADERS

David Haugen, Book Editor

BLACKBIRCH®
PRESS

THOMSON
———✳———
GALE

San Diego • Detroit • New York • San Francisco • Cleveland • New Haven, Conn. • Waterville, Maine • London • Munich

For more information, contact
The Gale Group, Inc.
27500 Drake Rd.
Farmington Hills, MI 48331-3535
Or you can visit our Internet site at http://www.gale.com

LIBRARY OF CONGRESS CATALOGING-IN-PUBLICATION DATA

Leaders / by David Haugen
    p. cm. — (Voices from the American Revolution)
Summary: A history of the Revolutionary War, as told through diary excerpts, letters, and personal narratives from American and British leaders and other eyewitnesses. Includes index.
  ISBN 1-4103-0414-0 (lib. bdg. : alk. paper)

Printed in the United States
10 9 8 7 6 5 4 3 2 1

CONTENTS

A TEST OF LEADERSHIP

In April 1775, after American minutemen traded shots with British troops at Lexington and Concord, the colonial legislatures called together the Second Continental Congress. Aware that a peaceful settlement of their differences with England was now dashed, the congressmen busied themselves with the necessities of war. They authorized the raising of a Continental army and they selected a man to lead it. That man was a forty-three-year-old Virginia planter named George Washington.

Washington was not a renowned military tactician when he was appointed to the post. Two decades earlier, he had served in the French and Indian War as a major and then a colonel, but his rather minor exploits were more often failures than successes. Washington, however, had political backers who praised the young officer's eagerness, and a published account of his early military adventures was widely read. The men of the Second Continental Congress were certainly familiar with Washington's deeds, and they were acquainted with his pedigree. Washington was a trustworthy, close-mouthed gentleman who earned the respect of those he met. More importantly, though, he hailed from Virginia.

This seemingly unimportant fact is often cited as one of the deciding factors that helped the Congress vote Washington into the post of commander-in-chief of the army. Their reasoning was quite logical. The major protests against England before the war were led by New Englanders, and the early stages of conflict centered on the town of Boston. In order to win the support of the southern colonies and make the cause a united struggle for independence, many New England congressmen agreed that it would be diplomatically beneficial for a southerner to lead the Continental army. Washington, the Virginian, was given the chance to lead America's army, in part because of his place of birth.

During the Revolutionary War, Washington proved himself up to the task of commanding the colonial armies. Although he suffered many battlefield defeats, he always managed to save the bulk of his army to fight another day. His willingness to

---

Twenty years before he assumed command of the Continental army, George Washington served in the French and Indian War (pictured).

YOUNG WASHINGTON'S FIRST BATTLE

take risks also paid off in the great strategic successes at the Battle of Trenton, New Jersey (1776), and at the final victory at Yorktown, Virginia (1781). The retired soldier with a spotty military record from the French and Indian War had, by 1781, become one of the most celebrated leaders in recent history.

Washington's story was not unlike that of many other patriot commanders during the Revolution. Some were veterans of past conflicts; others were completely untrained military men who rose to the occasion. General Horatio Gates, the hero of the Battle of Saratoga (1777), had been a soldier during the French and Indian War. Nathanael Greene was a Rhode Island assemblyman before the war started, but as a brigadier general in the Continental army, he quickly won the esteem of George Washington during the defense of New York in 1776. Greene continued to show promise in subsequent battles and in 1780 was given overall command of colonial forces fighting in the southern colonies.

Many of America's political leaders who, unlike Nathanael Greene, remained with their colonial legislatures or joined the newly formed Continental Congress were not novices in their roles. John Adams was a lawyer who had written criticisms of the Stamp Act, one of the chief pieces of parliamentary legislation that provoked the colonists to cry "tyranny" against the British Crown. In 1770, he became a member of the Massachusetts legislature. He would remain a public servant for nearly thirty years. Some colonial statesmen like John Hancock, however, were not lawmakers by training. Hancock had been a businessman before taking up the patriot cause and being appointed to the Continental Congress in 1774. Benjamin Franklin was also a tradesman before becoming a politician. Franklin, a printer, was elected to the Pennsylvania legislature in 1751. By the time he was appointed to the Continental Congress in 1775, he had more than two decades worth of political experience. Together, the members of the Continental Congress oversaw the conduct of the Revolutionary War, negotiations with foreign powers, and the completion of the peace treaty that gave the colonies their independence.

The British, who stood to lose from the bid for independence, were not initiates either to the political or the military aspects of war. King George III had been the monarch of England since 1760. His ministers and the members of the British Parliament were seasoned politicians who had managed the British Empire for some time. Few of these men thought that the taxes and laws that stirred the colonies to war were unfair or unfounded; most of the other nations within the empire had borne similar legislation without complaint. When war did come, these men had the power and resources to conduct it even though the battlefields were far across the Atlantic Ocean.

Britain's military leaders were also experienced men. The Seven Years' War (1756–1763) and its North American counterpart, the French and Indian War (1754–1763), had proved to be testing grounds for England's elite commanders. Lord Charles Cornwallis, the general who would have the ill fortune of losing to George

General Charles Cornwallis, who established himself as an elite military leader during the Seven Years' War, commanded British troops during the American Revolution.

Washington at Yorktown, had a distinguished career as a military leader fighting in Germany during the Seven Years' War. General William Howe had led troops at the Battle of Quebec (1759) during the French and Indian War. These men were professional soldiers who had been raised in a nation with a military tradition. Many were aristocrats, the sign of good breeding that allowed them to inherit the ranks of leadership. They looked with disdain at the ragtag, ill-trained, ill-equipped army that the colonies had fostered. With the well-disciplined troops under their commands, these British generals were able more often than not to sweep aside the rebel forces that opposed them.

Even with superior resources, experienced soldiers, and proven commanders, however, the British were unable to put down the colonial rebellion. In part, this was due to George Washington's leadership. His strategy of striking quick blows against the British army and then retreating before the enemy could overwhelm him with their superior numbers and expert soldiers kept the Continental army alive. It also wore down the British public's support for the war. In this manner, Washington used his often meager resources to great effect both on the battlefield and in swaying public opinion. George Washington, the relatively inexperienced Virginian, proved to be the superior leader, the man who could best the British Empire and win American independence.

CHRONOLOGY OF THE REVOLUTION

MARCH 1765

King George III of England approves the Stamp Act, which taxes the American colonies to help pay for the French and Indian War. Colonists protest the tax as unfair because it was levied without colonial representation in Parliament.

AUGUST 1768

Boston firebrand Samuel Adams calls for a boycott of English imports. In response, England sends troops to the colonies to maintain order.

MARCH 1770

Five colonists are killed after a brief confrontation with British soldiers outside Boston's Customs House. Known as the Boston Massacre, the event adds to the tensions in the colonies.

SEPTEMBER 1774

The colonies send delegates to the First Continental Congress to address the tensions between England and America.

JULY 1776

The Continental Congress votes to declare American independence. It adopts Thomas Jefferson's Declaration of Independence as its testimonial of British abuses and American resolve to be free.

DECEMBER 1776

Washington stages a daring surprise attack on Trenton, New Jersey, where Hessian mercenaries working for the British have camped for the winter.

OCTOBER 1777

While Washington fights battles in Pennsylvania, General Horatio Gates achieves a resounding victory over British general John Burgoyne's army near Saratoga, New York. Burgoyne's army is the first British command to surrender to patriot forces.

King George III of England

APRIL–AUGUST 1775

• The British commander in Boston sends units to nearby Lexington and Concord to seize colonial weapons and ammunition. The colonists are alerted to his move, and militia units from neighboring colonies converge on Concord to stop the British advance. The two sides exchange fire, and the British are forced to retreat back to Boston.

• The Continental Congress meets again to discuss breaking free from English rule. It appoints George Washington as the commander of military forces in America.

• Before Washington can arrive to take charge of the patriot units around Boston, the British advance and achieve a costly victory at the Battle of Bunker Hill.

• In August, after finally hearing of the skirmish at Lexington and Concord, King George III declares the colonies to be in revolt.

FEBRUARY 1778–JUNE 1779

• Benjamin Franklin helps broker a formal military alliance between France and America.

• France declares war on England.

• Spain officially declares war on England.

JULY–OCTOBER 1781

French troops arrive in Rhode Island. Their commander, the Comte de Rochambeau, persuades Washington to stage an offensive in the South against British forces under Lord Charles Cornwallis. With the French fleet cutting off Cornwallis's retreat by sea, the combined American and French armies surround the British army at Yorktown, Virginia, and force Cornwallis to surrender on October 19.

SEPTEMBER 1783

The Treaty of Paris is signed and the war ends, despite the fact that the Continental Congress would not finish ratifying the treaty until the following year. In November, George Washington resigns his commission as head of the Continental army.

George Washington

KING GEORGE III

Proclaiming the Colonies in Rebellion

*Tensions between England and the American colonies had been mounting for
some time before the Revolution began. Britain's Parliament—with the king's
blessing—had imposed several taxes and restrictive measures on the colonies. Many
colonists believed any such taxes or laws were unfair since Americans were not
represented in Parliament. The colonists made their opposition known through
formal complaints to the English government. Parliament, however, remained
convinced that it had a right to govern the colonies as it wished.*

   *Feeling that their opinions were being ignored, several colonials began to
accuse England's King George III of tyranny. The king sent troops to Boston,
Massachusetts—the town with the most outspoken critics of British rule—to keep the
rebellious mood from spreading. On April 19, 1775, a unit of British troops from
Boston marched toward nearby Concord to hunt for colonial weapons stores and two
main spokesmen of American discontent. At Lexington, Massachusetts, the soldiers
were halted by colonial minutemen determined not to let the British reach Concord.
Musket fire erupted, and the colonials fled. More colonials met the British at Concord and successfully turned the British back toward Boston with many casualties.
When King George III received word that British troops had been fired upon by
Americans, he issued the following proclamation that the American colonies were in
rebellion against the Crown. In his proclamation, the king urges his loyal soldiers and
civilians in the colonies to use any means to suppress the rebellion. He encourages his
loyal subjects to report to British authorities any information on colonists who might
be allied with the rebel cause. Word of the decree did not reach the colonies until
October 31, more than two months after it was drafted in England.*

Whereas many of our subjects in . . . North . . . America . . . have at length
proceeded to open an avowed rebellion, by arraying themselves in a hostile
manner . . . and traitorously preparing, ordering and levying war against us: And
whereas, there is reason to apprehend that such rebellion hath been much promoted
and encouraged by the traitorous correspondence, counsels and comfort of divers
wicked and desperate persons within this realm: To the end therefore, that none of
our subjects may neglect or violate their duty through ignorance thereof, or through
any doubt of the protection which the law will afford to their loyalty and zeal, we . . .
issue our Royal Proclamation, hereby declaring, that not only all our Officers, civil

and military, are obliged to exert their utmost endeavours to suppress such rebellion, and to bring the traitors to justice, but that all our subjects of this Realm . . . are bound by law to be aiding and assisting in the suppression of such rebellion, and to disclose and make known all traitorous conspiracies . . . and we do accordingly strictly charge and command all our Officers, as well civil as military, and all others our obedient and loyal subjects, to use their utmost endeavours to withstand and suppress such rebellion, and to disclose and make known all treasons and traitorous conspiracies . . . and for that purpose, that they transmit to one of our principal Secretaries of State, or other proper officer, due and full information of all persons who shall be found carrying on correspondence with, or in any manner or degree aiding or abetting the persons now in open arms and rebellion against our Government, within any of our Colonies and Plantations in North America, in order to bring to condign punishment the authors, perpetrators, and abetters of such traitorous designs.

Given at our Court at St. James's the twenty-third day of August, one thousand seven hundred and seventy-five, in the fifteenth year of our reign.

God save the King.

King George III, A Proclamation by the King for Suppressing Rebellion and Sedition, August 23, 1775.

When King George III imposed heavy taxes and restrictions on America, colonials began to accuse the monarch of tyranny.

Glossary

- **arraying:** displaying
- **levying:** imposing
- **apprehend:** believe
- **divers:** various
- **abetting:** assisting
- **condign:** deserved

ETHAN ALLEN

The Capture of Fort Ticonderoga

Although the colonial forces had won their first victories at Lexington and Concord, they were still badly in need of weapons—especially heavy cannons—if they were to match themselves against the British in Boston. Lieutenant Colonel Benedict Arnold of the Continental army believed the colonials could get what they

Ethan Allen and Benedict Arnold surprised and captured the commander of Fort Ticonderoga.

needed from Fort Ticonderoga, a poorly manned outpost 150 miles from Boston on the shores of Lake Champlain. Arnold learned that Ethan Allen, another colonel who had been organizing a ragtag group of Vermont farmers into a militia unit, had the same idea and planned to undertake the mission immediately. Arnold asked Allen and his Green Mountain Boys to serve under his command, but Allen's men refused to obey anyone but their leader.

Eventually Arnold and Allen made a joint assault upon the fort on May 10, 1775. The colonials surprised the British defenders and captured the fort's commander. They also seized one hundred cannons which were later used during the siege of Boston. Ethan Allen described his part in the attack in an autobiography published in 1779.

It was with the utmost difficulty that I procured boats to cross the lake. However, I landed eighty-three men near the garrison, and sent the boats back for the rear guard, commanded by Colonel Seth Warner; but the day began to dawn, and I found myself under necessity to attack the fort before the rear could cross the lake; and, as it was viewed hazardous, I harangued the officers and soldiers in the manner following:

"Friends and fellow-soldiers, You have, for a number of years past been a scourge and terror to arbitrary power. Your valor has been famed abroad, and acknowledged, as appears by the advice and orders to me . . . surprise and take the garrison now before us. I now propose to advance before you, and, in person, conduct you through the wicket-gate; for we must this morning either quit our pretensions to valor, or possess ourselves of this fortress in a few minutes; and, inasmuch as it is a desperate attempt, which none but the bravest of men dare undertake, I do not urge it on any contrary to his will. You that will undertake voluntarily, poise your firelocks."

The men being, at this time, drawn up in three ranks, each poised his firelock. I . . . marched them immediately to the wicket-gate aforesaid, where I found a sentry posted, who instantly snapped his fusee at me; I ran immediately toward him, and he retreated . . . within the garrison, gave a halloo, and ran under a bomb-proof. My party, who followed me into the fort, I formed . . . to face the two barracks which faced each other.

The garrison being asleep, except the sentries, we gave three huzzas which greatly surprised them. One of the sentries made a pass at one of my officers with a charged bayonet, and slightly wounded him. My first thought was to kill him with my sword; but, in an instant, I altered the design and fury of the blow to a slight cut on the side of the head, upon which he dropped his gun, and asked quarter, which I readily granted him, and demanded of him the place where the commanding officer kept. He showed me a pair of stairs in the front of a barrack, on the west part of the garrison, which led up to a second story in said barrack, to which I immediately repaired, and ordered the commander, Captain De la Place, to come forth instantly, or I would sacrifice the whole garrison; at which the Captain came immediately to the door, with his breeches in his hand. When I ordered him to deliver me the fort instantly, he asked me by what authority I demanded it. I answered him, "In the name of the great Jehovah, and the Continental Congress."

The authority of the Congress being very little known at that time, he began to speak again; but I interrupted him, and with my drawn sword over his head, again demanded an immediate surrender of the garrison; with which he then complied, and ordered his men to be forthwith paraded without arms, as he had given up the garrison.

Ethan Allen, *Narrative of Colonel Ethan Allen's Captivity, from the Time of His Being Taken by the British, near Montreal, on the 25th Day of September, in the Year 1775, to the Time of His Exchange, on the 6th Day of May, 1778.* Boston: Draper and Folsom, 1779.

Glossary

- **procured:** obtained
- **harangued:** addressed
- **arbitrary:** unrestrained
- **pretensions:** self-important airs
- **poise:** aim
- **firelocks:** muskets
- **fusee:** flintlock gun
- **haloo:** alarm shout
- **bomb-proof:** covered fortification
- **huzzas:** cheers
- **bayonet:** long blade attached to a musket
- **quarter:** mercy
- **breeches:** pants
- **arms:** weapons

WILLIAM HOWE

The Costly Victory at Bunker Hill

In May 1775, the British garrison in Boston finally received enough reinforcements from England to begin an attack against the rebel forces arranged on the high ground that encircled the city. Along with the needed men and supplies came three British generals—William Howe, John Burgoyne, and Henry Clinton. All three generals were convinced that the poorly disciplined colonial army could easily be brushed aside by the well-trained British regulars. The British plans, therefore, called for a frontal charge up Breed's Hill where the rebels appeared the strongest. On the morning of June 17, 1775, the British troops crossed the Charles River and began their assault. To their surprise, the rebel forces had fortified themselves quite well along the hillside, and the patriot defenders fought off two successive charges with relative ease. General William Howe personally led the British on the two failed charges. After the second attempt, many of his officers begged him to not to try another frontal attack. The hillside was already littered with British dead and injured. Howe, however, was headstrong and, supplied with reinforcements, routed the patriots on the third charge. After the bloody battle, which was named after nearby Bunker Hill, Howe became more sober about his losses. In this letter to a confidant, Howe—though never blaming himself for the costly victory—acknowledges how unwise the attack was and how few troops were now left to defend Boston.

Glossary

- **Entre nous:** French phrase meaning "between us"
- **I have heard a bird sing:** an anonymous person in power has told me

I freely confess to you, when I look to the consequences of it, in the loss of so many brave officers, I do it with horror. The success is too dearly bought. Our killed, serjeants and rank and file, about 160; 300 wounded and in hospital, with as many more incapable of present duty. The Rebels left near 100 killed and 30 wounded, but I have this morning learnt from a deserter from them that they had 300 killed and a great number wounded.

We took five pieces of cannon, and their numbers are said to have been near 6,000, but I do not suppose they had more than between 4 and 5,000 engaged. . . .

Entre nous, I have heard a bird sing that we can do no more this campaign than endeavour to

Although William Howe led his troops to victory in the Battle of Bunker Hill, both British and rebel forces suffered heavy losses.

preserve the town of Boston, which it is supposed the Rebels mean to destroy by fire or sword or both—and it is my opinion, with the strength we shall have collected here upon the arrival of the 4 battalions last from Ireland . . ., that we must not risk . . . the loss of Boston—tho' should anything offer in our favour, I should hope we may not let pass the opportunity [to attack].

The intentions of these wretches are to fortify every post in our way; wait to be attacked at every one, having their rear secure, destroying as many of us as they can before they set out to their next strong situation, and, in this defensive mode . . . they must in the end get the better of our small numbers. We can not . . . muster more now than 3,400 rank and file for duty, including the Marines, and the three last regiments from Ireland.

William Howe, "Assessment of the Battle of Bunker Hill, 1775." In Sir John Fortescue, ed., *The Correspondence of King George the Third, from 1760 to December 1783.* 6 vols. London: Macmillan 1927–1928. Courtesy of Librarian, Windsor Castle.

JOHN ADAMS

Nominating Washington as General-in-Chief

The Continental Congress met for a second time in May 1775. It had been less than a month since the first shots of the war were fired at Lexington and Concord. Unlike the meeting of the First Continental Congress, the delegates at the Second Continental Congress were no longer debating how to mend the situation with

John Adams

England. Instead, they were figuring out how the colonies could conduct a war against such a powerful enemy. First, the colonies needed an army, so Congress quickly authorized the creation of one. Second, the new army would need a leader, a general who would be responsible for the overall military progress of the war. In June, John Adams, a delegate from Massachusetts, nominated a Virginia planter named George Washington. Washington had been an officer in the French and Indian War, but he did not possess as much experience as other possible candidates for the position of general-in-chief.

In the following selection from his autobiography, Adams describes the events surrounding his nomination of Washington. He mentions how John Hancock, the president of the Continental Congress, also had a desire to be nominated for the generalship. Adams recounts how Hancock revealed his humiliation when Adams's cousin, Samuel Adams, seconded Washington's nomination and brought the subject to open debate. Although some delegates objected to Washington's appointment, eventually enough members supported the choice, and Washington became the general-in-chief of the newly formed Continental army.

Mr. Hancock himself had an ambition to be appointed commander-in-chief. Whether he thought an election a compliment due to him, and intended to have the honor of declining it, or whether he would have accepted, I know not. To the compliment he had some pretensions, for, at that time, his exertions, sacrifices and general merits in the cause of his country had been incomparably greater than those of Colonel Washington. But the delicacy of his health, and his entire want of experience in actual service . . . were decisive objections to him in my mind. . . .

Accordingly, when Congress had assembled, I rose in my place, and in as short a speech as the subject would admit, represented the state of the Colonies, the uncertainty in the minds of the people, their great expectation and anxiety, the distresses of the army, the danger of its dissolution, the difficulty of collecting another, and the probability that the British army would take advantage of our delays, march out of Boston, and spread desolation as far as they could go. I concluded with a motion . . . that Congress would adopt the army at Cambridge, and appoint a General; that though this was not the proper time to nominate a General, yet, as I had reason to believe this was a point of the greatest difficulty, I had no hesitation to declare that I had but one gentleman in my mind for that important command, and that was a gentleman from Virginia who was among us and very well known to all of us, a gentleman whose skill and experience as an officer, whose independent fortune, great talents, and excellent universal character would command the approbation of all America, and unite the cordial exertions of all the Colonies better than any other person in the Union.

Glossary

- **pretensions:** deserving claims
- **want of:** lack of
- **dissolution:** disbanding
- **desolation:** destruction
- **motion:** proposal
- **adopt:** take charge of
- **Cambridge:** town just outside of Boston
- **approbation:** approval
- **cordial:** friendly
- **allude:** refer
- **countenance:** facial expression
- **mortification:** humiliation
- **physiognomy:** facial expression

Mr. Washington, who happened to sit near the door, as soon as he heard me allude to him, from his usual modesty darted into the library-room. Mr. Hancock—who was our President, which gave me an opportunity to observe his countenance while I was speaking on the state of the Colonies, the army at Cambridge, and the enemy—heard me with visible pleasure; but when I came to describe Washington for the commander, I never remarked a more sudden and striking change of countenance. Mortification and resentment were expressed as forcibly as his face could exhibit them. Mr. Samuel Adams seconded the motion, and that did not soften the President's physiognomy at all.

Charles Francis Adams, ed., *The Works of John Adams, Second President of the United States: With a Life of the Author, Notes and Illustrations.* 10 vols. Boston: Little, Brown, 1850–1856.

GEORGE WASHINGTON

A Reluctance to Assume Command

On June 15, 1775, the Second Continental Congress made the momentous decision to appoint George Washington to lead the as yet nonexistent Continental army. Washington accepted the position reluctantly. In this letter to his wife, Martha (known affectionately as Patsy), the new general of the Continental army writes of his anxieties in taking command.

You may believe me, my dear Patsy, when I assure you, in the most solemn manner, that, so far from seeking this appointment, I have used every endeavor in my power to avoid it, not only from my unwillingness to part with you and the family, but from a consciousness of its being a trust too great for my capacity, and that I should enjoy more real happiness in one month with you at home, than I have the most distant prospect of finding abroad, if my stay were to be seven times seven years. But as it has been a kind of destiny that has thrown me upon this service, I shall hope that my undertaking it is designed to answer some good purpose. You might, and I suppose did perceive, from the tenor of my letters, that I was apprehensive I could not avoid this appointment, as I did not pretend to intimate when I should return. That was the case. It was utterly out of my power to refuse this appointment, without exposing my character to such censures, as would have reflected dishonor upon myself, and given pain to my friends. This, I am sure, could not, and ought not, to be pleasing to you, and must have lessened me considerably in my own esteem. I shall rely, therefore, confidently on that Providence, which has heretofore preserved and been bountiful to me, not doubting but that I shall return safe to you in the fall. I shall feel no pain from the toil or the danger of the campaign; my unhappiness will flow from the uneasiness I know you will feel from being left alone.

Glossary

- **solemn:** serious
- **tenor:** tone, mood
- **intimate:** hint
- **censures:** blame

George Washington, farewell letter to Martha Washington, June 18, 1775, in John C. Fitzpatrick, ed., *The Writings of George Washington, from the Original Manuscript Sources, 1745–1799.* 39 vols. Washington, DC: U.S. Government Printing Office, 1931–1944.

GEORGE CLINTON

The Importance of Small Victories

*In 1776, British General William Howe launched a campaign in New England
to secure major waterways. One of his principle objectives was the port city of New
York. George Washington sought to delay Howe from reaching his goal, but despite
some attempts at resistance around the city, the patriot army was never strong
enough to hold back the British. In the following account, patriot general George
Clinton describes a skirmish on Manhattan Island on September 16, 1776. Since
the patriots had been losing battles ever since the war began, Clinton considers the
small victory in this firefight to be an important boost to patriot morale.*

On Monday morning, about ten o'clock, a party of the enemy . . . attacked our
advanced party. . . . They were opposed with spirit, and soon made to retreat
to a clear field . . . where they lodged themselves behind a fence covered with bushes.
Our people attacked them in front, and caused them to retreat a second time, leaving
five dead on the spot. We pursued them to a buckwheat field on the top of a high
hill, distant about four hundred paces, where they received a considerable reinforcement, with several field-pieces, and there made a stand. A very brisk action ensued at
this place, which continued about two hours. Our people at length worsted them a
third time, caused them to fall back into an orchard, from thence across a hollow, and
up another hill not far distant from their own lines. A large column of the enemy's
army being at this time discovered to be in motion, and the ground we then occupied
being rather disadvantageous . . . our party was therefore ordered in, and the enemy
was well contented to hold the last ground we drove them to. . . .

I consider our success in this small affair, at this
time, almost equal to a victory. It has animated our
troops, gave them new spirits, and erased every bad
impression the retreat from Long Island, had left on
their minds. They find they are able, with inferior
numbers, to drive their enemy, and think of nothing now but conquest.

Glossary

- **field-pieces:** cannons
- **worsted:** beat

Albert Bushnell Hart, ed., *American History Told
by Contemporaries*, vol. 2, *Building of the Republic*.
New York: Macmillan, 1899.

NATHANAEL GREENE

Independence Is America's Cause

In January 1776, Thomas Paine published a small pamphlet called Common Sense. *The work attempted, in plain language, to explain why England and the American colonies should be separated.* Common Sense *became hugely popular in America because it reinforced the growing sentiment that independence was the answer to colonial ills.*

On January 4, five days before Paine's pamphlet was published, General Nathanael Greene wrote the following letter to Samuel Ward, a member of the Continental Congress. At the time, Congress was undecided on how it could conduct a war since it had so little money to afford weapons, uniforms, food, and other items necessary to equip an army. The members of Congress spent so much time deliberating on this topic that the military leaders feared their soldiers would never receive the needed supplies. Greene argues that the cause of liberty is worth any expense and that continual deliberation must be set aside in favor of immediate action. He also suggests that the Congress adopt a declaration of independence, a document that would give reasons for the conflict between England and the colonies and promote liberty as a common cause. Greene's thoughts on independence and the pressing need for action were shared by many Americans at the time, and this widespread endorsement of rebellion explains why Common Sense *found such a receptive audience in the colonies.*

Permit me . . . to recommend from the sincerity of my heart, ready at all times to bleed in my country's cause, a declaration of independence; and call upon the world, and the great God who governs it, to witness the necessity, propriety and rectitude thereof.

My worthy friend, the interests of mankind hang upon that truly worthy body of which you are a member. You stand the representatives not of America only, but of the whole world; the friends of liberty, and the supporters of the rights of Human Nature.

How will posterity, millions yet unborn, bless the memory of those brave patriots who are now hastening the consummation of Freedom, Truth and Religion! But want of decision renders wisdom in council insignificant, as want of power hath prevented us here from destroying the mercenary troops now in Boston. . . . How can we, then, startle at the idea of expense, when our whole property, our dearest connexions, our

Nathanael Greene urged Congress to declare America's independence and to take the military action needed to win it.

liberty, nay! life itself is at stake? Let us, therefore, act like men inspired with a resolution that nothing but the frowns of Heaven shall conquer us. It is no time for deliberation; the hour is swiftly rolling on when the plains of America will be deluged with human blood. Resolves, declarations and all the parade of heroism in words will not obtain a victory. Arms and ammunition are as necessary as men and must be had at the expense of everything short of Britain's claims.

Peter Force, ed., *American Archives: Fourth Series, Containing a Documentary History of the English Colonies in North America from the King's Message to Parliament of March 7, 1774 to the Declaration of Independence by the United States.* 6 vols. Washington: M. St. Clair Clarke and Peter Force, 1837–1846.

Glossary

- **rectitude:** righteousness
- **worthy body:** Congress
- **consummation:** achievement
- **mercenary:** hired
- **want of:** lack of
- **deluged:** flooded

GEORGE WASHINGTON

Surprising the Hessians at Trenton

Washington led a surprise raid on Trenton, New Jersey, on Christmas night 1776.

Throughout the campaigns of 1775, George Washington had suffered several defeats at the hands of the British. With his small, unprofessional army, Washington had been fighting a defensive war—holding off British advances in the New England colonies and then withdrawing his army when it looked as though he would be overwhelmed by the enemy. By the winter of 1776, Washington was eager to repair America's fighting reputation. He planned an attack on two New Jersey villages where British general William Howe had stationed some of his Hessian mercenaries—German soldiers paid to fight for England. Washington devised a bold plan to strike the enemy when they least expected. He organized seven thousand men in Pennsylvania and intended to have them ferried across the Delaware River to make a surprise raid upon the Hessians at Trenton and Bordentown, New Jersey. He scheduled the attack for Christmas night, assuming that the Hessians would be celebrating and unprepared for military action.

The evening of December 25 was cold and snowy. It took many hours for Washington's troops to get across the ice-filled Delaware, but their surprise upon the Hessians was complete. Two colonial forces converged on Trenton while another advanced on Bordentown in the early hours of December 26. The Germans sprang from their barracks and guard posts only to be shot down or captured by the Americans. In all the Hessians suffered 50 casualties and lost another 920 men as prisoners. Washington sent off a quick dispatch to John Hancock, president of the Continental Congress, informing him of the great victory.

I have the pleasure of congratulating you upon the success of an enterprise, which I had formed against a detachment of the enemy lying at Trenton, and which was executed yesterday morning. The evening of the twenty-fifth I ordered the troops intended for this service to parade back to McKonkey's Ferry, that they might begin to pass as soon as it grew dark, imagining we should be able to throw them all over, with the necessary artillery, by twelve o'clock, and that we might easily arrive at Trenton by five in the morning, the distance being about nine miles. But the quantity of ice, made that night, impeded the passage of the boats so much, that it was three o'clock before the artillery could all be got over; and near four before the troops took up their line of march. This made me despair of surprising the town, as I well knew we could not reach it before the day was fairly broke. But as I was certain there was no making a retreat without being discovered and harassed on repassing the river, I determined to push on at all events. I formed my detachment into two divisions, one to march by the lower or river road, the other by the upper or Pennington road. As the divisions had nearly the same distance to march, I ordered each of them, immediately upon forcing the out-guards, to push directly into the town, that they might charge the enemy before they had time to form.

The upper division arrived at the enemy's advanced posts exactly at eight o'clock; and in three minutes after, I found, from the fire on the lower road, that the divisions had also got up. The out-guards made but small opposition, though, for their numbers, they behaved very well, keeping up a constant retreating fire from behind houses. We presently saw their main body formed; but, from their motions, they seemed undetermined how to act. Being hard pressed by our troops, who had already got possession of their artillery, they attempted to file off by a road on their right, leading to Princeton. But, perceiving their intention, I threw a body of troops in their way, which immediately checked them. Finding from our disposition, that they were surrounded, and that they must inevitably be cut to pieces if they made any further resistance, they agreed to lay down their arms. The number that submitted in this manner was twenty-three officers and eight hundred and eighty six men. Colonel Rahl, the commanding officer, and seven others were found wounded in the town. I do not exactly know how many were killed; but I fancy twenty or thirty, as they never made any regular stand. Our loss is very trifling indeed, only two officers and one or two privates wounded.

George Washington, report to John Hancock on the victory at Trenton, December 1776. In John C. Fitzpatrick, ed., *The Writings of George Washington, from the Original Manuscript Sources, 1745–1799.* 39 vols. Washington, DC: U.S. Government Printing Office, 1931–1944.

- **executed:** carried out
- **impeded:** slowed
- **repassing:** recrossing
- **out-guards:** sentries
- **checked:** halted
- **submitted:** surrendered

BENJAMIN FRANKLIN AND SILAS DEANE

Take the Fight to the Enemy's Door

To secure its independence, America needed the aid of foreign powers. France was the nation most willing to help the revolutionaries, primarily because France and England had been rivals for many years. In 1776, France began secretly sending arms, munitions, and money to the colonies. Two years later, the Continental Congress sent an official delegation to the court of King Louis XVI to negotiate a formal treaty with France. Seventy-year-old Benjamin Franklin and Silas Deane were two of three men assigned to this diplomatic mission.

Being so close to Britain, the American diplomatic team knew of the British public's growing reluctance to pursue the costly war. In May 1777, Franklin and Deane sent the following letter back to the Continental Congress. In it, the diplomats suggested that the Americans send a few fighting ships into the shipping lanes used by the British merchant fleet. It was Franklin and Deane's hope that disrupting some of Britain's trade would increase the British people's discontent with the war. The diplomats expected that the attacks would be a complete surprise and thus have a good chance of success. They even hinted that a seaborne invasion of a city in the British homeland might shock the enemy to sue for peace. Regardless, Franklin and Deane argue that any attacks on England's merchant fleet would be useful since captured cargo could be used back in the colonies to help continue the war.

The colonial fleet, however, was never large enough to send many ships into the sea-lanes around England. Franklin and Deane's plan was not practical, and the Revolution continued to be fought almost exclusively in North America.

We have not the least doubt but that two or three of the Continental frigates sent into the German Ocean, with some lesser swift sailing cruisers, might intercept and seize great part of the Baltic and Northern trade, could they be in those seas by the middle of August, at farthest; and the prizes will consist of articles of the utmost consequence to the States. One frigate would be sufficient to destroy the whole of the Greenland whale fishery, or take the Hudson Bay ships returning. . . .

A blow might be struck that would alarm and shake Great Britain and its credit to the centre. The thought may appear bold and extravagant, yet we have seen as

Benjamin Franklin suggested that American naval forces attack the British merchant fleet.

Glossary

- **frigates:** fast fighting ships
- **German Ocean:** North Sea
- **swift sailing cruisers:** smaller but faster fighting ships
- **prizes:** captured enemy cargo
- **extravagant:** too costly and too risky
- **in consequence:** therefore
- **Liverpool:** a city in England
- **Glasgow:** a city in Scotland
- **a million of treasure:** a lot of money
- **on the continent:** in America
- **stores:** supplies
- **capital:** excellent

extraordinary events within these two years past as that of carrying the war to our enemy's doors. As it appears extravagant, it would be in consequence unexpected by them, and the more easily executed. The burning or plundering of Liverpool, or Glasgow, would do more essential service than a million of treasure and much blood spent on the continent. It would raise our reputation to the highest pitch, and lessen in the same degree that of our enemy's. We are confident it is practicable, and with very little danger, but times may alter with the arrival of the frigates, yet in that case their cruise on this coast bids fairer to be profitable than any other, and they may at least carry back in safety many of the stores wanted, which is a most capital objects, should the other be laid aside.

Francis Wharton, ed., *The Revolutionary Diplomatic Correspondence of the United States*. 6 vols. Washington, DC: U.S. Government Printing Office, 1889.

JOHN PAUL JONES

The Bon Homme Richard's Victory

Although the Revolutionary War was not characterized by naval conflict, one sea battle that took place in 1779 has become legendary. The Bon Homme Richard, a converted cargo ship captained by patriot John Paul Jones, was sailing off the coast of Britain looking for merchant ships to seize or sink. On September 23, the colonial vessel was trailing a fleet of merchantmen when their fighting escort ship, the Serapis, turned to engage. Jones quickly learned that his larger-caliber cannons had a tendency to explode when fired, so he decided to sail in close and ram the British warship. The maneuver was a success, and the two ships fought a confusing, entangled battle. At one point, Lieutenant Richard Dales, in command of a section of colonial cannons, heard the British captain hail the Bon Homme Richard and ask if the colonials had struck their colors—that is, run up their flag as a sign of surrender. As Dale recorded in his account of the battle, John Paul Jones is said to have given his famous reply, "I have not yet begun to fight." In his own official report of the action, excerpted below, Jones blames the cowardice of three of his junior officers as leading to the confusion surrounding the striking of the Bon Homme Richard's colors. According to Jones, the officers called to the British ship and announced that the Americans wished to

Patriot John Paul Jones

surrender. Jones does not mention the exact words of his defiant response to the British captain when asked if this surrender was authentic, but he does describe the fury of the battle that followed his reply. After four hours of combat, the colonial sailors boarded the Serapis *and forced the British to surrender. The* Bon Homme Richard *was too badly damaged to maintain its seaworthiness, so Jones had his men transfer to the* Serapis *and sail for a French port. The* Bon Homme Richard *sank on September 25.*

I directed the fire of one of the three [remaining] cannon against the [*Serapis's*] main-mast, with double-headed shot, while the other two were exceedingly well served with grape and canister shot to silence the enemy's musketry, and clear her decks, which was at last effected.

The enemy were, as I have since understood, on the instant of calling for quarters when the cowardice or treachery of three of my under officers induced them to call to the enemy. The English commodore asked me if I demanded quarters; and, I having answered him in the most determined negative, they renewed the battle with double fury. They were unable to stand the deck; but the fire of their cannon, especially the lower battery, which was entirely formed of 18-pounders, was incessant. Both ships were set on fire in various places, and the scene was dreadful beyond the reach of language. To account for the timidity of my three under officers—I mean the gunner, the carpenter, and the master-at-arms—I must observe that the two first were slightly wounded; and, as the ship had received various shots under water, and one of the pumps being shot away, the carpenter expressed his fear that she would sink, and the other two concluded that she was sinking, which occasioned the gunner to run aft on the poop without my knowledge to strike the colors. Fortunately for me, a cannon ball had done that before by carrying away the ensign staff. He was therefore reduced to the necessity of sinking, as he supposed, or of calling for quarter; and he preferred the latter.

John Paul Jones, The Capture of the *Serapis* by the *Bon Homme Richard,* 1779.

MARQUIS DE LAFAYETTE

A Frenchman's View of America

Twenty-year-old Marie-Joseph-Paul-Yves-Roch-Gilbert du Motier, the Marquis de Lafayette, was a French officer who arrived in the American colonies in 1777. Lafayette admired George Washington, and he volunteered to serve in the Continental army without pay in the hope that Washington would see fit to honor him with his own command. Lafayette and Washington did become friends, and Washington quickly gave the Frenchman a leadership position. Lafayette remained a loyal friend of the patriots. His enthusiasm for America is evident in this excerpt from a letter he wrote to his wife just after arriving in the colonies. Lafayette paints a very rosy—if not completely accurate—image of American society as he saw it.

Glossary

- **cultivated:** practiced
- **healths:** toasts

I will now tell you about the country and its inhabitants. They are as agreeable as my enthusiasm had painted them. Simplicity of manners, kindness, love of country and of liberty, and a delightful equality everywhere prevail. The wealthiest man and the poorest are on a level; and, although there are some large fortunes, I challenge any one to discover the slightest difference between the manners of these two classes respectively towards each other. I first saw the country life at the house of Major Huger. I am now in the city, where everything is very much after the English fashion, except that there is more simplicity, equality, cordiality, and courtesy here than in England. The city of Charleston is one of the handsomest and best built, and its inhabitants among the most agreeable, that I have ever seen. The American women are very pretty, simple in their manners, and exhibit a neatness, which is everywhere cultivated even more studiously than in England. What most charms me is, that all the citizens are brethren. In America, there are no poor, nor even what we call peasantry. Each individual has his own honest property, and the same rights as the most wealthy landed proprietor. . . .

As to my own reception, it has been most agreeable in every quarter. . . . I have just passed five hours at a grand dinner, given in honor of me by an individual of this city. Generals Howe and Moultrie, and several officers of my suite, were present. We drank healths and tried to talk English.

Marquis de Lafayette, letter to his wife, 1777.

CHARLES CORNWALLIS

Surrender at Yorktown

During the first few months of 1781, George Washington learned that the French fleet would be sailing in the region of the Chesapeake Bay. Washington decided to move his army out of New York and plan a trap for a large portion of the British army that was encamped in Yorktown, Virginia. Combining his army with French land forces in the area, Washington hoped to surround the port city and, using the French fleet, cut it off from escape or reinforcement by sea. The plan worked flawlessly. On September 26, Washington arrived outside Yorktown. With more than sixteen thousand colonial and French soldiers, he laid siege to the seventy-four hundred British troops and German mercenaries that were sheltered within the well-prepared trenches and fortifications of the city. As the siege wore on through the early weeks of October, General Charles Cornwallis, the British commander, understood the predicament of his army. Because he was cut off from all supplies, his food stores ran low. Disease and casualties took their toll on his men. On October 14, the American and French forces captured the last two defensive redoubts—or fortified positions—that guarded Yorktown. On October 16, Cornwallis tried unsuccessfully to evacuate his troops across a river. With his last plan dashed, he sent officers out the following day to discuss terms for surrendering his army. On October 20, Cornwallis wrote the following report to Clinton in which he summarized the events of the battle that made his surrender inevitable.

On the evening of the 14th [the colonial and French forces] assaulted and carried two redoubts that had been advanced about 300 yards for the purpose of delaying their approaches, and covering our left flank, and during the night included them in their second parallel, on which they continued to work with the utmost exertion. Being perfectly sensible that our works could not stand many hours after the opening of the batteries of that parallel, we not only continued a constant fire with all our mortars and every gun that could be brought to bear upon it, but a little before daybreak on the morning of the 16th, I ordered a sortie of about 350 men, under the direction of Lieut.- Colonel Abercrombie, to attack two batteries which appeared to be in the greatest forwardness, and to spike the guns. . . .

This action, though extremely honorable to the officers and soldiers who executed it, proved of little public advantage, for the cannon having been spiked in a hurry, were soon rendered fit for service again, and before dark the whole parallel and

When colonial and French forces cut off supplies to British troops in Yorktown, General Cornwallis (right) was forced to surrender to Washington (left).

batteries appeared to be nearly complete. At this time we knew that there was no part of the whole front attacked on which we could show a single gun, and our shells were nearly expended. . . .

Our numbers had been diminished by the enemy's fire, but particularly by sickness, and the strength and spirits of those in the works were much exhausted, by the fatigue of constant watching and unremitting duty. Under all these circumstances, I thought it would have been wanton and inhuman to the last degree to sacrifice the lives of this small body of gallant soldiers, who had ever behaved with so much fidelity and courage, by exposing them to an assault which, from the numbers and precautions of the enemy, could not fail to succeed. I therefore proposed to capitulate; and I have the honor to enclose to your Excellency the copy of the correspondence between General Washington and me on that subject, and the terms of capitulation agreed upon. I sincerely lament that better could not be obtained, but I have neglected nothing in my power to alleviate the misfortune and distress of both officers and soldiers. The men are well clothed and provided with necessaries, and I trust will be regularly supplied by the means of the officers that are permitted to remain with them.

Charles Cornwallis, report to Sir Henry Clinton on the Battle of Yorktown, October 20, 1781.

Glossary

- **parallel:** a trench dug alongside an enemy trench
- **batteries:** artillery
- **mortars:** small cannons
- **sortie:** raid
- **in the greatest forwardness:** closest
- **spike the guns:** make the cannons unusable
- **unremitting:** unrelieved
- **fidelity:** loyalty
- **alleviate:** lessen

FOR MORE INFORMATION

Books

Kenneth C. Davis, *Don't Know Much About George Washington*. New York: HarperCollins Juvenile, 2002.

Jean Fritz, *Why Not, Lafayette?* New York: Puffin, 1999.

Daniel E. Harmon, *Lord Cornwallis: British General*. Philadelphia: Chelsea House, 2001.

Bonnie L. Lukes, *John Adams: Public Servant*. Greensboro, NC: Morgan Reynolds, 2000.

Web Sites

The History Place: The American Revolution
www.historyplace.com
One of the many topics covered by The History Place Web site, this series of pages on the Revolution presents time lines of the era. On each time line page, visitors can access information that relates to the period between early colonization and 1790.

Kid Info: American Revolution
www.kidinfo.com
This Web site gathers links to other sites devoted to some aspect of the Revolution. This is a good place to track down further information on a specific topic of interest.

Liberty: The American Revolution
www.pbs.org
A companion to the PBS documentary miniseries on the Revolution, this Web site is an excellent resource for students.

Index